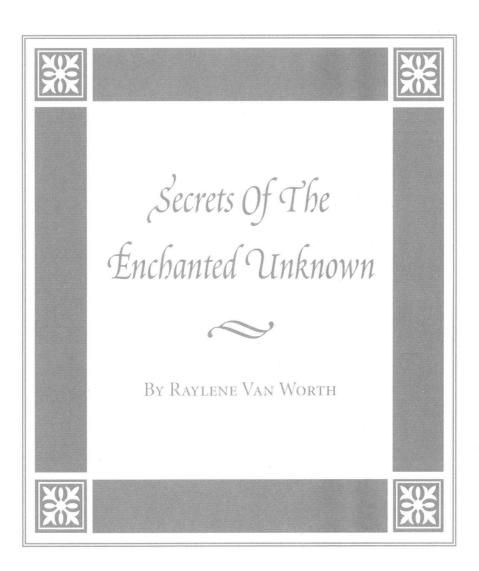

# Secrets Of The Enchanted Unknown

## By Raylene Van Worth

# ✠ CONTENTS ✠

## Introduction

## Chapter One: Enchantments for Love

## Chapter Two: Enchantments for Personal Power and Success

# Chapter Three: Enchantments for Prosperity

# Chapter Four: Enchantments for Health

# Conclusion

The enchanted world around us is full of secrets, secrets that, upon telling, open us to a greater, fuller life than we ever thought possible. The very stars, stones and flowers we see every day can teach us how to live in harmony with nature and gain new power over ourselves and our circumstances.

In ancient times, these secrets were passed down from generation to generation, with every family compiling its own formulas for love, success, wealth, health and happiness that let its members lead contented, successful lives. Charms of love, rituals for success and abundance, curative recipes... all these were tucked away in special Books of Secret Enchantments and guarded jealously from the eyes of strangers.

These days, such secrets have been lost as people lead hectic lives far from their families and ancestral homes. That's why I am so glad to be able to share my Secrets of the Enchanted World with you. I hope you will pass it down to future generations in your family, adding any charms, lore and recipes that may have been given you by your ancestors. Guard it well, and keep it from the eyes of strangers. Keep your eyes open to the magic around you, and this book can become a treasured heirloom, a guide to happiness and success as you travel the great magical road of life.

## Entering the World of Enchantments

You may be making your first few furtive steps along the magical road into the world of enchantments. If this is so, I'm sure you'll be delighted with the new sights, brilliant colors, and breathtaking vistas that you'll discover there. Don't forget that the most radiant view you'll ever take in is what you see in the light of your Spiritual Self, the source of all enchantments.

Here is some information and tips about the various magical tools — candle rituals, moon rituals, flower and herbal secrets — you will use to advance along your path into the world of enchantments.

## ᴗ: Secrets of Candle Rituals

However simple a ritual may be, preparation is all-important. If you are going to burn candles, as you will here, you must have a safe place to burn them. It must be somewhere they can remain undisturbed, for many rituals must be done over a period of days. It must be someplace with no risk of fire — no filmy curtains or diaphanous drapery. Also, this place must be quiet and free from distraction — with no stereos, televisions, pets or children who can knock things over. A basement or attic is ideal.

You will need something such as a chest, a box, a table or even the floor. A small, low coffee table or a card table is perfect. Cover the table with a white cloth. You will also need a number of candle-holders. Choose small ones so when you use several candles at one time the altar will not become cluttered; this is not only for aesthetic reasons but for reasons of fire safety as well.

Incense is a great aid to atmosphere and concentration. In ancient days it was believed that the smoke of incense carried prayers to the gods. Any incense will do, although frankincense, sandalwood and pine are traditional. However, if you are doing a ritual for which you know there is a corre=sponding fragrant herb, you may use incense with that scent to enhance the procedure.

You should always do ritual work on an empty stomach, as this forces the spirit to a higher level. Also, you should be cleansed. Take a dip in a bath to which has been added a handful of salt (sea salt is ideal). This is not the time to add magical herbs to your bath; at this point you are cleansing and purifying yourself, creating a blank slate onto which you will write your purpose. Cool, but not uncomfortably cold water is desirable, and remember not to use soap. Use the time you spend in this bath to meditate on the pur=pose of your work.

The candles may be of any type; it is the color that is important. Candles that are to be used for magic must be "dressed" with oil. You can use special anointing oils found in occult shops, which will be specific to the purpose of your ritual; you can use essential oils of flowers and herbs; or you can use plain olive oil. To dress a candle, you anoint it with the oil, rubbing it into the candle from the center towards one end, then from the center towards the other. Always rub the candles in the same direction — from the center out. While doing so, you should concentrate on the purpose of your magic work. After that, if you wish, you may scratch your name into the candle that will represent yourself.

Two white candles, known as the altar candles, are always on the table, placed on the two far corners and lit before any others. Other candles vary according to the ritual. Always light the candles in the order indicated in the ritual, and extinguish them in reverse order. You may also place on the altar a symbol of the deity of your choice, if you wish.

Use the candle rituals in this book as a guide to create your own rituals to help you attain your desires.

## ◡ Secrets of Moon Rituals

The mystique of the Moon. At times you may marvel at its perfectly circular splendor. At other times you may watch its crescent shape float across the sky. The beautiful and mysterious power of the Moon plays an important role in the world of enchantments.

You can harness the magical energy of the Moon and use it to your benefit. Above all, you should treat the marvelous force of the Moon with respect and wonder. Gaze at it, get to know its different phases, reflect on its beauty and splendor that has inspired poets for thousands of years.

Follow carefully the instructions for the Moon Rituals in this book. They will give you access to lunar power and will help you take an active role in bettering your life and filling it with the glow of love, success, abundance and health.

One helpful instrument for performing Moon rituals is a Moonstone. Possessing one will help you to create and maintain a strong connection to the Moon; it is the strength of this connection that will help you achieve your goals. Have your Moonstone with you when you perform these rituals, and it will gradually absorb the soft light of the Moon as well as of your Spirit, and so will gain more magical power.

## Secrets of Numerology

Numbers are ancient and remarkable. As far back in time and in history as we can go, we can find the traces of divination methods based on numbers. The Chinese Ha-Do, Arabic Geomancy, the Egyptian Tarot, the Hebrew Cabala, and of course, the Chinese I-Ching (the oldest known book of divination), are all linked to fairly complex arithmetic processes.

There are no unlucky numbers once we know their exact meaning and learn to use them wisely. They all contribute to life's harmony and to success. Transforming letters or astrological events into numbers, as we do in this book, has been a sacred ritual for thousands of years, so these numerological instructions should be scrupulously followed.

You'll soon discover that the numerological keys in this book will help bring your personality to light. For example, they can reveal to you your true underlying self, the unrecognized subtleties of your hidden psyche and the laws governing your love life.

Indeed, the power of numbers is truly universal, and all numbers have powers you can use to your advantage. Their crisp efficiency hides much mysterious knowledge and many wonders, as you'll soon see.

## ∴ Secrets of Plants and Herbs

We are all intimately involved with plants. Even if you have a "black thumb" and can't grow a garden or so much as a cactus, you must interact with plants every day in order to live. Any vegetable, grain or fruit you eat is, of course, a plant; plants also feed the animals that give us meat. Even the very oxygen we breathe comes to us from plants. It is therefore vital that we treat them with respect and learn their secrets.

In addition to their uses for decoration, shade and food, plants have very important spiritual and healing powers. You may not be aware of it, but many essential medicines that you're used to seeing in synthetic form originally came from plants. The chemical found in common aspirin comes from the inner bark of the white willow tree. Digitalis, a significant heart stimulant, was originally synthesized from the leaves of the garden foxglove. It is estimated that up to 75% of our current useful medicines were discovered in the rain forests of South America, Africa and Asia.

It is critical to note that certain herbal remedies can be dangerous if used without supervision. Those which the Secrets of the Enchanted Unknown recommends have been used as household cures for untold generations and are generally safe if you follow the directions indicated; any questionable substances will be noted. If you feel uneasy about any remedy suggested here, simply don't use it. There are qualified herbal medicine practitioners who can help you, or you can ask your doctor for advice.

# Secrets of Magical Recipes

The kitchen is one of the most magical places in the home. Some recipes have magic put into them on purpose. You can use the enchanting properties of vegetables, fruits, and herbs to create delectable dishes with a little magic sprinkled in! I've included some of my favorites at the end of each chapter, but feel free to become a "magical chef" yourself and create your own tasty recipes.

The most important part of magic work is to believe in what you are doing. If you just do the actions and say the words mechanically, the ritual will not work. The purpose must be from your heart. Don't be discouraged if everything you want doesn't materialize immediately. As with all rituals, practice makes perfect; you will probably feel your skills and concentration sharpen with each ritual you perform. Have patience, faith, and most of all respect for the natural world, and you will feel yourself becoming more and more attuned to the magic of the world of enchantments.

# CHAPTER
## ONE

*Enchantments for Love*

*I*n fairy tales,
when we read that the handsome prince
sweeps the beautiful maiden off her feet with a flourish,
we smile and sigh, knowing
they will "live happily ever after."
And sometimes love can be that simple... but usually
it's much more complicated! In fact, the only thing we know
for sure about love
is that it's still the greatest mystery of all!

❧

Since the beginning of history,
people have worried about love just as much as we do today.
Magical means to attract, deepen, and keep love alive
have been collected by cultures the world-over for thousands
of years. It seems everybody needs a little help now and then
when it comes to affairs of the heart!

❧

In the following time-tested rituals,
you can use the secrets of herbs, the mystery of candles,
the magic of numbers or the beauty
of the Moon to help you find the love you're seeking.

*Nearly every pagan pantheon has contained at least one deity who personified the power of love and/or presided over marriage. While it would be impossible to tell you about them all, following is a description of some of the most famous gods and goddesses of love. The next time you need a "shoulder to cry on" when dealing with matters of love, invoke one of these deities and tell them your troubles.*

**Aphrodite** is the ancient Greek goddess of love and beauty. Romans called her Venus. She was said to be notoriously unfaithful to her husband, Hephaestus, and her many lovers. Her sacred colors are white, green, blue and scarlet. Her sacred love-drawing gem is lapis lazuli; trees sacred to her are myrtle, myrrh and palm. The word "aphrodisiac" comes from her name. She was the personification of passion, and only later did the idea of spiritual love come under her domain. Because she was said to have risen from the sea, many of her temples were on the ocean shores.

**Astarte** is the supreme female deity of the Phoenicians. She symbolizes love, fruitfulness and the female principle. She is depicted as a woman robed in flames, armed with a bow and sword, and wearing the horns of a cow on her head to symbolize her powers of fertility. She often carries either a serpent or a child.

**Belili** is the Sumerian goddess of love who preceded Astarte. She is also a lunar goddess, a goddess of trees, wells and springs, and ruler of the Underworld.

**Creirwy** is the Celtic goddess of love and beauty. According to Celtic mythology, Creirwy was the most beautiful woman in the world, and her brother Avaggdu was the ugliest man.

**Freya** is the Norse goddess of love, beauty and healing. She is the consort of the sunshine god Odur and the sister of Frey, lord of peace and prosperity. Her golden chariot is drawn by white cats. Amber is sacred to her, as are cats and falcons, and Friday is named after her.

**Frigga** is another Norse goddess who was the patronness of marriage and fecundity. Her eleven handmaidens help her reunite lost lovers and preside over married love. Keys are her symbols and rams are sacred to her.

**Hathor** is the ancient Egyptian goddess of love, beauty and mirth, the patronness of women, infants, marriage and music, and symbol of the female principle. She was also worshipped as a lunar goddess and fertility goddess. She is seen as a woman with the head of a cow, wearing between her crescent horns the headdress of two plumes and a solar disk decorated with stars.

**Hera** was the Greek goddess of wedlock, women and childbirth, queen of Olympus and the heavens. Hers was a jealous wrath against her philandering husband, Zeus. Romans called her Juno.

**Inanna** is an ancient Sumerian goddess of love and war, a mother goddess and queen of heaven. She came to be associated with the Babylonian goddess Ishtar. Her symbol is the bundle of reeds. A great epic poem was written about her descent to the Underworld.

**Ishtar** had two aspects: She was the gentle, loving, compassionate goddess of love and fertility; she was also a war goddess so cruel, aggressive and lustful that the gods trembled when warriors sang her praise. Her sacred animal was the lion; the Tree of Life was her symbol, and her womb was believed to be the never-ending source of the water of life.

**Aizen Myo-o** is the Japanese god of love and beauty who represents loving passion transformed into the quest for illumination. He is depicted as having three eyes and six arms, a ferocious face crowned by a lion's head and a thunderbolt that calms evil passions and guilty desires. Despite his threatening appearance, he is filled with compassion.

**Angus** is the Celtic god of love and beauty, the patron of youths and maidens. He was known for his beauty and his golden hair. On his harp of gold, he played romantic melodies, and his kisses turned into bright birds that hovered protectively over the heads of young lovers.

**Cupid,** also known as Eros, was originally portrayed as a handsome youth, but later became best known as a winged infant. He was the son of Venus, and went armed with a magic bow and arrows which he shot as "darts of love" into the hearts of mortals.

**Hyacinthus** is an ancient god of Spring and flowers, worshipped in Crete, Mycenae and Sparta, who was the lover of Apollo. The flower bearing his name is said to have sprung from his blood.

**Kama** is the Hindu god of love and the personification of desire. Neither humans nor gods can resist his advances, and he is endowed with eternal youth. He carries a sugarcane bow with a bowstring of bees and arrows tipped with flowers.

Since the beginning of time, people have attempted to formulate potions to induce love and stir flagging desire. Some of the best stimulants of this type are naturally occurring foods like oysters, onions, ginseng and ginger. But if the subtle effect of these substances isn't enough for you, try one of these potions.

One warning: it is against the principles of "good/white magic" to try to impose your will on another person by magical means — even for such a benevolent reason as to induce true love. If you do so, remember the old saying: "Be careful of what you ask for; you might get it." The spell in the potion could rebound — you could find *yourself* falling in love (or desiring) someone completely unexpected or unsuitable; the person you work the spell on could become obsessed with you; or you may find that someone you don't desire has used a similar potion on *you*. It may be best to use these potions as an offering to the gods and goddesses of love, asking them to please send you your heart's desire. That way, you are not using the potion to bend the will of one specific person, and you may find your true love in a completely unexpected way.

# Love Perfume

Add to a bottle of your favorite perfume or cologne
a few drops of musk oil, a pinch of ground coral, cantharides
("Spanish fly"), brown sugar, cinnamon and rose petals.
Shake well and then place the bottle in front of an image
of your desired lover (or your chosen deity of Love)
for five days and nights.

To attract a lover, rub some of the magical love perfume on
your forehead, breasts, and feet.

✽

# Love Potion #1

Fill a small pot with a handful of rosemary leaves, thirteen
anise seeds, two cloves, three rose geranium leaves, a tablespoon of honey and some grapefruit juice. Place the pot over
a fire and bring the brew to a boil. Strain the mixture
through a sieve. Add some of the liquid to a glass of wine or
fruit juice, and then serve it to the man or woman from
whom you desire love, or use it as an offering.

✽

# Love Potion #2

*1 cup water*
*1/4 cup grapefruit juice*
*1 teaspoon fennel*
*1 teaspoon vervain*
*3 pinches of nutmeg*

Place all ingredients into a pot over a fire
and bring it to a boil. Sit before the pot with a pink candle
and concentrate on the man or woman from whom you
wish love, chanting his or her name out loud for thirteen
minutes. Remove the pot from the fire and strain the potion
through a cheesecloth. Add a bit of honey to sweeten the
potion, and give it to the one you desire.

Note: Be sure to prepare it on a Friday night.

🌺 If you sneeze on a Tuesday, you will kiss a stranger.

🌺 If you sneeze on a Saturday, you will see your true love on the following day.

🌺 If two lovers sneeze at the same time, it is an omen of good fortune.

🌺 To give your lover a handkerchief as a gift means that you will soon part and never marry.

🌺 Itchy lips are a sign that you will soon be kissed. If the right side of your body itches, it is a sign that a lover is thinking about you. An itchy nose indicates a secret admirer.

Love letters should always be written in ink and mailed on Fridays (the day of the week ruled by Venus, the goddess of love).

It is unlucky to mail love letters on Sunday, Christmas Day, February 29, and September 1.

Setting fire to a love letter will bring an end to the love affair; however, if you burn one of your lover's letters, the size and color of the flames will enable you to determine whether or not your lover has been faithful and true to you. If the flames burn high and light–colored, the love is strong; if the flames burn weak and blue, the love affair is doomed.

If your hand trembles while you write a love letter, it is a good sign that means your love is reciprocated. If the ink blots, it means that your loved one is thinking fond thoughts of you.

To receive a love letter that is insufficiently stamped is an omen that the love affair is coming to an end. The same applies to love letters that arrive damaged or with the flaps open.

# To Open Yourself To Love

*Remember that two white candles, called the altar candles,
are always on the table, placed on the two far corners and lit before any others.
In this ritual, in addition to the altar candles, a white candle representing
yourself and incense, you will need one red candle, one orange candle
and one pink candle. Arrange the red on the left and the pink on the right of the
white candle, with the orange above the white candle.*

*Step 1* ❧ Light altar candles and incense.

*Step 2* ❧ Sit for a few minutes, imagining yourself with a new love in your life.

*Step 3* ❧ Light the white candle, concentrating on yourself, and say, *"This candle holds the spark of my spirit, worthy of love, open to love."*

*Step 4* ❧ Light the red candle, concentrating on passion. Say, *"May this flame bring the heat of passion to my life. May it bring me love that burns brightly and long. May it open me to the world of my senses so I may see the love around me."*

*Step 5* ❧ Light the pink candle, concentrating on romance. Say, *"May this flame bring the blush of romance to my life. May it bring me true and tender love with the highest ideals. May it open me to the world of my emotions so I may see the love around me."*

*Step 6* ❧ Light the orange candle, concentrating on attraction. Say, *"May this flame draw love to me, who is worthy of love and ready to give love in return. May this love be true, passionate and lasting. May it draw closer to me every day."*

*Step 7* ❧ Imagine your new love. See yourself happy and content. See this love as true and lasting, passionate and tender, healthy and worthy. Say, *"All love is sweet, given or returned. Common as light is love, and its familiar voice wearies not ever. Love alters not with hours or weeks, but lasts even until the edge of doom."*

*Step 8* ❧ Think now of your wish fulfilled. Say, *"This new Love now is mine. I hold it and have it, and now it fills my need. I have received it safely and am glad. Ever is it thus. Now all is well."*

*Step 9* ❧ Sit quietly for five minutes and let the candles and incense burn.

*Step 10* ❧ Say, *"As I have willed this, so may it be done."*

Repeat this ritual the following day.

## Aphrodisiac Sachet

*You need a Full Moon in order for this ritual to be effective. Collect an herb mixture of verbena, lemon and elder flowers in the center of a square of red felt or cotton. Gather up the ends and tie them together with red wool yarn or cotton twine. Place this powerful love sachet under your pillow or carry it on your person.*

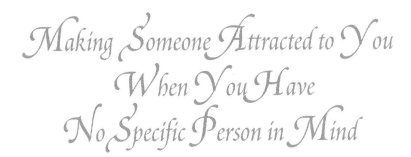

## Making Someone Attracted to You When You Have No Specific Person in Mind

You need a Waxing Moon for this spell. At sunset on a Friday, cast any three of the following herbs into a blazing hearth fire (or bonfire, if outdoors): basil, catnip, coriander, ginger, jasmine, powdered juniper berries, lavender, lovage, rosemary, rose petals, violets or yarrow. While the herbs are burning, recite the following magical incantation:

*My true love's face*
*I've yet to see*
*I know not what*
*His (her) name will be*
*But soon his (her) heart*
*will beat for me.*
*Come hither, my love.*
*So may it be.*

## Attracting Love with the Moonstone

In order to accomplish this ritual, you will need to perform it on the night of the Full Moon. Have a Moonstone by your side. Place it between two red or pink candles. When you light the candles, anoint the stone with a drop of musk oil and say the following:

*Stone of the Moon*
*Which attracts love and desire*
*I consecrate thee as a tool*
*Of love and magic.*
*And in the sacred name*
*Of the goddess*
*I charge thee now*
*With love-drawing power.*
*So may it be!*

Carry this consecrated Moonstone on your person during the day (in a pocket, purse or charm bag). It is a powerful love-drawing amulet. At night, sleep with it under your pillow.

# Your Love Number

Your Love Number can tell you precious information about your feelings and your sexuality. This number is determined by your astrological sun sign. The following table lists the astrological sun signs and their corresponding Love Numbers. After you have discovered your astrological Love Number, turn to the following Love Number Interpretations. Your Love Number might reveal some profound and unexpected insights about your emotions and sexuality.

## ❧ ASTROLOGICAL LOVE NUMBERS ☙

| | | | |
|---|---|---|---|
| CAPRICORN | ♑ | December 21 to January 20 | 8 |
| AQUARIUS | ♒ | January 21 to February 20 | 7 |
| PISCES | ♓ | February 21 to March 20 | 9 |
| ARIES | ♈ | March 21 to April 20 | 3 |
| TAURUS | ♉ | April 21 to May 20 | 6 |
| GEMINI | ♊ | May 21 to June 20 | 4 |
| CANCER | ♋ | June 21 to July 20 | 2 |
| LEO | ♌ | July 21 to August 20 | 1 |
| VIRGO | ♍ | August 21 to September 20 | 4 |
| LIBRA | ♎ | September 21 to October 20 | 6 |
| SCORPIO | ♏ | October 21 to November 20 | 3 |
| SAGITTARIUS | ♐ | November 21 to December 20 | 5 |

# Love Number Interpretations

**1.** As a number 1, the primary characteristic of your sexuality, which is controlled by the sun, is clearly a tendency to be "dominant." Depending on the partner with whom you share sexual relations, obstacles to happiness can arise quickly because of this characteristic. It seems that you always, even unconsciously, seek to impose your own view of the relationship in question. Let's clarify this: it doesn't mean that you demonstrate brusqueness in your sexual behavior. Dominant doesn't mean domineering! The nuance is important. For example, if you prefer certain sex games more than others, you make an effort to lead your partner into responding to your wishes. That's what can complicate your relationships. Try to remedy this by attempting to interpret your partner's desires. You'll find that you get real pleasure out of satisfying them because your "dominant" nature will discover a certain sense of superiority at having uncovered your partner's "secrets" and then freely consenting to play along with them. But it is nonetheless essential that you find a partner who, while submissive, is still creative and exciting in this domain. It's paradoxical, but indispensable for your sexual fulfillment.

**2.** Number 2, you make a perfect spouse — warm and affectionate, desirous of making the relationship last and ready to overlook many little annoyances. Dramatic, and hypersensitive, you need a partner who can bring you back down to earth. You are as steadfast in your love as you are in friendship. You believe what people tell you without trying to verify their word. When it comes to expressing desire, remember that your partner can't read your mind, number 2. Don't be afraid to ask for what you want, and make sure that your wish to fulfill your partner's desires doesn't make you ignore your own.

**3.** Number 3, you are capable of deep and lasting love; nevertheless, you prefer to remain single. You are often considered fickle and undependable because, in fact, what you most love is to be loved. That's why you try so hard to create the perfect mood around you. When you are married, though, you know how to be loving and affectionate in a balanced and lasting manner. But be careful, number 3, of devoting yourself to other interests to the detriment of your home life. That would be a mistake.

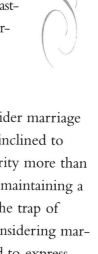

**4.** Number 4, you don't fall in love easily. You consider marriage as something not to be entered into lightly and are little inclined to show your feelings, especially in public. You require security more than romance, and while you are capable of entering into and maintaining a full, stable, loving relationship, don't let yourself fall into the trap of thinking with your wallet more than your heart when considering marriage. Learn to listen to your feelings, to accept them and to express them to your partner if you don't want to find yourself alone because "you never share yourself." Remember, not only is it okay to need another person, it's okay to let yourself play as well.

**5.** Number 5, your charm and magnetism attract admirers by the dozen. More sensual than sentimental, you can fall passionately in love, but only for a while. Marriage to number 5 is often a lottery: it's all good or all bad. But it also depends on your partner. If you are allowed to express your romanticism and affection and you are understood, you can be a wonderful spouse. If you're misunderstood, you'll become glum, silent and quick-tempered. Your great sensuality makes you a terrific partner in love. Don't be afraid to commit yourself to a relationship. If you watch yourself and don't give in to the impulse to run away the moment "the bloom is off the rose," your adventuresome spirit can bring great love and excitement to another person's life.

6. Number 6, you have fallen in love easily since you were young. Your love may be short-lived, but it is profound and intense. You may even seek love frantically when you are afraid of being stifled by an excess of tenderness and affection. You may be frightened by your own desires for harmony and "domestic bliss," but don't let yourself fall into the trap of thinking that "stable" equals "dull." There is something magical about a comfortable, sustained relationship. You have an emotional sensitivity and a tendency toward extreme behavior that may lead you to judge your loved ones by your own high standards. Remember that love is all give-and-take, that when two people each bring their own perspective to a relationship, their love becomes greater. Keeping that in mind, though, don't let your "pendulum personality" swing into making you a self-sacrificing martyr. Compromise and moderation are the rule. Take heart, number 6 — once you liberate your capacity for harmony in love, your relationship will be long, faithful, fruitful and happy.

7. Number 7, you often marry young or not at all. As you grow old, you find it more and more difficult to express your feelings and emotions. In any case, you're not very communicative or demonstrative. You're more attracted to intellectual pursuits than to marital bliss. You often let affairs of the heart fall by the wayside as your sharp intellect concentrates on one puzzle after another. Don't leave your loved ones behind; they are anxious for you to share yourself with them. Accept that the one you love may not have your fervor for ferreting out the mysteries of the universe. Number 7, everyone has their own intensity. Let your passion spill over into your

emotional relationship and you will discover a depth of love you never thought possible.

8. Number 8, you may live a great love affair on the condition that you are understood and your character is accepted unconditionally. You may be madly in love one day and shower your lover with gifts, thoughtfulness and affection, and the next day be completely withdrawn, absorbed in thought. It's not that you love your partner less, it's just part of your nature. However, it is also part of your nature to think about straying when your exacting standards are not met or you think you're being neglected. Don't let temptation carry you into a situation you really don't want. You require a partner who shares your opinion that a relationship is something to be invested in for the long term. Sex, companionship, affection — this is the "investment capital of love." Spend it wisely.

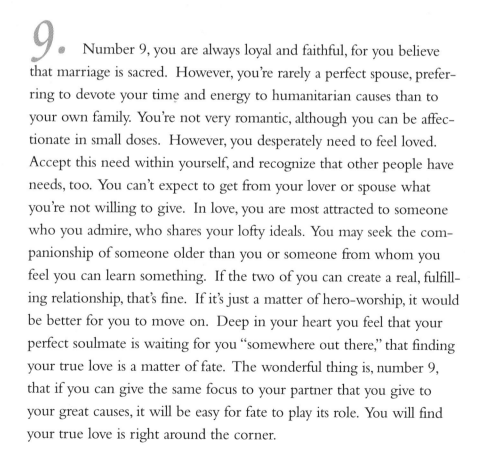

9. Number 9, you are always loyal and faithful, for you believe that marriage is sacred. However, you're rarely a perfect spouse, preferring to devote your time and energy to humanitarian causes than to your own family. You're not very romantic, although you can be affectionate in small doses. However, you desperately need to feel loved. Accept this need within yourself, and recognize that other people have needs, too. You can't expect to get from your lover or spouse what you're not willing to give. In love, you are most attracted to someone who you admire, who shares your lofty ideals. You may seek the companionship of someone older than you or someone from whom you feel you can learn something. If the two of you can create a real, fulfilling relationship, that's fine. If it's just a matter of hero-worship, it would be better for you to move on. Deep in your heart you feel that your perfect soulmate is waiting for you "somewhere out there," that finding your true love is a matter of fate. The wonderful thing is, number 9, that if you can give the same focus to your partner that you give to your great causes, it will be easy for fate to play its role. You will find your true love is right around the corner.

*In the Victorian language of flowers, the following plants symbolize the various aspects of love.*

*Keep these magical qualities in mind when offering a bouquet to a special someone.*

**Acacia** . . . . . . . . . . . . . . . . . . Platonic love

**Ambrosia** . . . . . . . . . . . . . . Love returned

**Batchelor's Buttons** . . . . . . . . Hope in love

**Bridal Rose** . . . . . . . . . . . . . . Happy love

**Cabbage Rose** . . . . . . . Ambassador of love

**Carolina Rose** . . . . . . . . . . Dangers of love

**Honey Flower** . . . . . . . Sweet and secret love

**Honeysuckle** . . . . . . . . . . . . Bonds of love

**Lemon Blossoms** . . . . . . . . Fidelity in love

**Linden Flower** . . . . . . . . . . Conjugal love

**Lotus** . . . . . . . . . . . . . . . . . Estranged love

**Moss** . . . . . . . . . . . . . . . . . Maternal love

**Myrtle** . . . . . . . . . . . . . . Love and fertility

**Pink Carnation** . . . . . . . . . . Women's love

**Purple Lilac** . . . . . . . First emotions of love

**Red Catchfly** . . . . . . . . . . . . Youthful love

**Red Tulip** . . . . . . . . . . . Declaration of love

**Rose** . . . . . . . . . . . . . . . Love and marriage

**Thornless Rose** . . . . . . . . Early attachment

**Toothwart** . . . . . . . . . . . . . . . Secret love

**Yellow Rose** . . . . . Decrease of love; jealousy

**Yellow Tulip** . . . . . . . . . . . . Hopeless love

**Colors** must also be considered when one is planning a romantic encounter. Each color and even each shade of one color sends out certain kinds of vibrations able to influence our psyche. Here again, magic had preceded science. Since ancient times, colors were taken into account during each magic ceremony.

To give you a more concrete idea of the real effect of the colors on behavior, here is a famous experiment performed in the United States on the advice of the famous Professor Alexander Schauss, eminent researcher in photobiology at Tacoma, Washington University:

A prison cell from the US Navy Prison in Seattle was painted pink. Placed in this bizarre-colored cell were the most difficult prisoners. In fifteen minutes, the worst prisoner became as gentle as newborn babies!

The explanation given by Professor Schauss was that the quality of the vibration emitted by the pink color acted directly on the adrenaline glands and their hormones that stimulate the nervous system. From this stimulus, the rate of the adrenaline slows down and consequently, the degree of excitement.

Following is an analysis of people and their reactions to color. For example, when you are dressing for a date or redecorating your home, use these colors to create your desired effect.

| | |
|---|---|
| *blue* | The color of equilibrium. It gives back the taste for life and helps depressed people to overcome the idea of suicide. Blue also helps digestion. |
| *navy blue* | A color not recommended for use, since it increases the tendency for selfishness and indifference, and may induce depression. |
| *light blue* | A color that calms and slows down fears of the future. It favors optimism. This color is advised for young children and fragile psychological types. Think about this color for wallpaper for a child's room and for their clothes. |
| *red* | This color is excitement personified. A shocking color for sex and seduction. If your room is wallpapered red you will increase your seductive power enormously. It is the color of love, violent passion and life. |
| *dark red* | This color incites fights but creates some bizarre and disturbed reflexes. Placed side-by-side with black, it can trigger ideas of hate and vengeance. Be careful. |
| *pink* | Symbolizing relaxation, it helps to bring sleep and calms the nerves. To a person's equilibrium it brings goodness and indulgence. |
| *yellow* | Everything moves with this color. It tones the body and the spirit and helps intellectual work and concentration. |
| *orange* | It calms impulsiveness and discourages tricksterism. It makes one inclined to think about one's decisions. It brings a true self-control and maintains the pressure in the effort. |

It favors shyness and modesty. But, on the other hand, it develops the artistic sense, the taste for the beautiful and the quiet life.

*light green*

It insists on prudence and sometimes self-centeredness. It makes one become tough at gambling and thirsty for material things. It increases sexual appetite. This is both a positive and negative color... using it is a difficult choice to make.

*dark green*

The color of passivity and indolence. It develops the "art" of putting it off to the next day. It is, however, an excellent calming color.

*grey*

The red in purple promotes enthusiasm for life, as well as ambition. The blue in purple slows down excess and favors discussion. A fine color for most purposes.

*purple*

It brings pure luck, peace and calm.

*white*

Carefulness and wisdom are favored by this color, which increases equilibrium and constancy in effort.

*black*

*After you've dressed yourself in "the colors of love," you might enjoy inviting a special someone over to share dessert. Here are two Magical Recipes for Love...*

*The brilliant red color of the raspberries*
*in the first recipe and the cherries in the second symbolize heartfelt passion.*

## Romantic Raspberry-Guava Pie

Pastry for a 10-inch, 2-crust pie
4 cups fresh raspberries
4 cups chopped guava fruit
1 cup brown sugar

1/2 cup flour
1/2 teaspoon ginger
1/2 teaspoon allspice
2 tablespoons margarine, softened

Preheat the oven to 425°F. Mix the raspberries, guava fruit, brown sugar, flour, ginger and allspice in a medium-sized bowl. Line a 10-inch pie pan with the bottom layer of the pastry, and pour the raspberry mixture into it. Dot with the margarine. Cover with the top crust and seal the edges. Make several slits in the top crust. Bake 35-45 minutes, or until the crust is brown and the juices have begun to bubble through the slits in the top crust.

*Variation* ⌘ To really spark some passion, substitute passion fruit for the guava in the above recipe. You may also substitute strawberries for the raspberries if you so desire.

*Magical Qualities* ⌘ Abundant love, increasing passion, ardor, fertility and satisfying relationships.

## Cha-Cha Cherry Chill

1 (12-oz) can frozen cherry juice
2 cups apricot nectar
1 tablespoon sugar

1/2 teaspoon almond extract
Almonds and cherries for garnish

Prepare the juice according to can directions. Mix the cherry juice, apricot nectar, sugar and almond extract in a large freezer-proof bowl. Place bowl in freezer until the juice mixture is semi-solid. Be careful — don't leave it in the freezer too long or it will freeze too hard! When the mixture is semi-solid, transfer it to a blender or food processor and mix until it is very smooth. Pour into glasses; garnish with a whole almond and a cherry.

*Variation* ⌘ Frozen strawberries may be thawed and substituted for the cherry juice.

*Magical Qualities* ⌘ Fertility, love magic, sexual balancing and blending.

# CHAPTER TWO

# Enchantments for Personal Power and Success

*E*veryone wants to be successful in his or her chosen field,
regardless of age, gender, or culture. You can harness the power of all your
radiant positive qualities and use this power to achieve or further your own suc=
cess. One popular symbol of financial success in our society is the Diamond.
And in fact, the diamond symbolizes many of the qualities necessary for success.

❧

As you probably know, the diamond is the hardest, strongest substance
found in all of nature. The word "diamond" comes from the Greek word adamas,
meaning "invincible"; thus, it can impart to you the power of invincibility and
success. Keep the following image in mind as you pursue your
own success — a diamond withstands grinding and polishing, and through
them, releases its visual bonfire of inner radiance.

❧

So, the best investment you can make for success is to invest in
your own inner radiance — that is, your own true personality, personal power
and positive qualities. A recent study conducted in the United States concluded
that any individual's success depends 85% on his personality; only the remaining
15% represents his actual knowledge or experience in his chosen field. Think of
politicians: all over the world at election time, the majority of voters vote "for the
person," which really means the politician's personality. For your success,
too, your personality is the key.

❧

Just as it takes ages to turn coal into diamonds, releasing or recreating
the true brilliance of your inner personality takes time, too. Don't expect
immediate results. Use your intense inner power and magical tools to sculpt this
deep transformation within yourself for success.

*I*t is the rarity and beauty of stones, crystals and gems
that makes them precious, yet the most ordinary piece of quartz
can contain magic if you magnetize it properly. Stones represent the enduring gifts of
the spirit; magic worked with stones operates on deep levels of the spiritual world. They
are used like psychic batteries; they can be charged with a particular energy which is
stored and released later when needed.

Each stone, crystal and gem has its own special meaning,
its own realm of power. When you want a certain force to enter your life,
a good way to focus that force is to have on your person at all times the stone
governing that force. Wear it, sleep with it under your pillow, have it in the bath with
you (unless it would be damaged by the water) and rub it on your body. Meditate by
concentrating on your stone, and soon the force it represents
will pervade your life.

 *The Power of Gems*

| Stone | Properties |
| --- | --- |
| **Tiger's eye** | Strengthens character, banishes fears related to self |
| **Amethyst** | Develops spirituality |
| **Rose Quartz** | Heals |
| **Blue-laced Agate** | Promotes softness and femininity |
| **Botswana Agate** | Brings gifts and small pleasures |
| **Red Jasper** | Promotes earthly love and family feelings |
| **Ruby** | Increases high-voltage love and passion |

| Stone | Properties |
|-------|-----------|
| **Octahedron** | Channels energy into work |
| **Garnet** | Heightens sexual awareness |
| **Jade** | Brings beauty |
| **Opal** | Calls forth the spirits |
| **Turquoise** | Protects, maintains health and happiness |
| **Sapphire** | Gives peace of mind, favors enlightenment |
| **Emerald** | Aids future seeing |
| **Topaz** | Brings courage and warmth |
| **Lapis Lazuli** | Bestows children |
| **Petrified wood** | Clarifies legal matters and bureaucratic work |
| **Iron Pyrite** | Causes deception and misunderstanding |
| **Tektite** | Banishes, sucks up bad energies |
| **Aquamarine** | Clears the mind, cools, purifies |
| **Moss Agate** | Brings peace of mind, ends anxiety |
| **Rutilated Quartz** | Promotes creativity |
| **Agate with fossils** | Integrates riches, inheritances and sudden increases of wealth |
| **Bloodstone** | Injects strength, relieves depression |
| **Agate Geode** | Opens psychic powers |
| **Quartz Crystal** | Helps concentrate |
| **Diamond** | Bestows indomitable strength, everlasting ties |
| **Moonstone** | Invokes the magic of the night |
| **Brown Jasper** | Connects you to your body |
| **Amethystine Agate** | Encourages flexibility and change |
| **Gold** | Attracts abundance and richness |
| **Silver** | Makes you appreciate the purity and simplicity of poverty |

# Increasing Your Connection With the Power of the Moon

Celebrating the Full Moon is one way of attuning yourself to the Moon cycle; this will increase your personal power when performing the other rituals. Naturally, this ritual is to be performed at or around the time of the Full Moon. The closer you are to the exact night, the better. This celebration allows you to partake in the magical waxing and creation aspect of this cycle. The more people you have for this feast, the merrier. It helps the festivities if the participants dress for the occasion and decorate the space in a festive manner. The mood should be one of elfish magic, mystery, joy and power.

Prepare the food beforehand so things will run smoothly. Light incense and have brightly colored candles around. Festive folk music will also help set the mood. When everyone has arrived and before the actual feasting begins, have everyone sit in a circle and read the following text which was written as an homage to the Full Moon:

> This is the time of the fullness of the symbol of our Lady, the Moon. All things wax and wane, and on this evening, the powers of life, of magic and of creation are at their highest. This is the time of building and of doing. It is a time when the veil between the mundane world and the strange and beautiful realms of the magical unknown world becomes very thin indeed.

> There is a magnificence to this time. The ancients knew well the mysteries of this night and used them to build and strengthen themselves — as well as to partake of the elfish adventures of which we can have but little inkling. . .

> This is a time for weaving the inchoate into being, for spinning the strands of space and time to bring forth Creation. For all does rotate, and turn about verse and

*Mystery of the greatest magnitude. The gods knew of it, and we shall, also. Weave a spell of Moonlight, and fashion with it a flavor of pure magical substance.*

*There is a challenge and a joy to building and creating — the joyous strife of a just battle, the cascading passion of lovemaking. . . even birth pangs in creating a new life. There is the Peace of Aphrodite that follows — a thoroughly fulfilling quietude. And it is easy, really. Very easy and the most natural of things.*

*This is a time of traveling unseen in the full Moonlight, a time for hearing elfin music not made by humankind. It is a time for oneness with the forest, with the mountains, with the eternal and life-giving sea, with the warm rains and the bolt of lightning that creates the very spark of life.*

After sharing this text with all the participants, the festivities can begin. Bring out the food and enjoy the feast. Afterwards, move out the tables and dance the night away.

# Becoming Attuned to the Magic of the Full Moon

The Full Moon can be an unsettling time, as people often get a little crazy. However, did you know that it is possible to attune yourself to the magical power of the Moon? Start this ritual with the first quarter of the Moon. If you don't have one already, get yourself a Moonstone (it can be a piece of jewelry or just a loose stone you carry around in a small pouch on your person). Carry it with you day and night. It will work with those subtle energies that the Moon dispenses that have an effect on you.

During this period you may notice different things about yourself. Your behavior may change from what it usually is: If you are normally a social person, you may find yourself spending more time alone, or vice–versa. You may find that you are listening to a different kind of music or that your curiosity or interests are growing in new directions.

About a week before the Full Moon, start spending a little time with the Moon each evening (i.e., before you go to bed). Make yourself an herbal infusion (i.e., chamomile tea or another herbal tea that you may prefer). With your Moonstone by your side, seat yourself under the Moon — in the garden, on a balcony or at an open window. You do not have to do anything in particular — just sit with the Moon, absorbing its cool, mysterious light.

You will notice the changes in yourself and find yourself more attuned to the Moon. Having your Moonstone with you will recharge its energy. By the time the Moon is full again, you will find yourself welcoming the Moon's power and ready to use its magic.

❧ Since the time of the ancient sages, the power of colors has been used to focus the energy of the rainbow upon the adept user. Many mysteries, such as those of stones, plants and candles, depend in part on the power granted them by their color.

❧ Every culture has its guardian of the rainbow. Tibet has its Khandromas — sky-roving, rainbow-clad goddesses who attach themselves to the different colors of the spectrum. They can be lassoed with magic ropes and brought to earth to grant the powers of their particular color to anyone clever and strong enough to hold them. The Greeks worshipped Iris, goddess of the rainbow, who was messenger for the queen of the gods and led heroic travelers through the sky to the destination of their quest. In Norse mythology, the god Heimdal guarded Bifrost, the rainbow bridge leading to the heavenly halls of Valhalla.

❧ You can use the power of colors to invest yourself with the ancient secrets of the rainbow. Try an experiment: the next time you have an important meeting or appointment, choose the colors you wear according to the vibrations they emit. Have one principal color in your outfit and select your accent colors with care to complement the energy you wish to radiate. For example, a woman who has a major business presentation would do well to wear a vibrant purple suit to reward her ambition and bring her power in business, with a white blouse for sincerity and a gold scarf or jewelry to give her the power of affluence, persuasion and charm (wearing gold jewelry will also invest her with the power of the mineral gold itself). Does this seem like too "loud" an outfit for you? Imagine the same woman wearing mousy brown and beige. Which woman seems more confident, more capable of controlling a business?

❧ Just as colors can influence those around you to your benefit, they can influence you, as well. For example, the next time you are feeling run-down or tired, surround yourself with the color red. It will help summon your reserves of energy in order to accomplish a task. Meditate upon the color blue to feel more tranquil and patient — just make sure it's not too dark a blue, for that may lead you to depression. Everyone knows that red means energy, blue means tranquillity, yellow means happiness and green means prosperity, but who knows where these meanings come from? That is the secret of the rainbow.

## ∽ THE POWER OF COLORS ∽

| | |
|---|---|
| **WHITE** | *Purity, truth, sincerity, healing, peace, totality. White protects and purifies the entire body and soul* |
| **RED** | *Strength, health, vigor, sexual love, energy, expansion, power, daring, survival, activity, movement, passion, fast action and stimulation* |
| **BLUE** | *Tranquillity, understanding, patience, health, peace, impulsiveness, communication, truthfulness, self-knowledge, strength of will, depression and changeability (in very dark shades)* |
| **GREEN** | *Finance, fertility, luck, regeneration, rest, repair* |
| **GOLD** | *Knowledge, mental activity, attraction, persuasion, charm, confidence* |
| **YELLOW** | *Attraction, spirituality, clairvoyance, happiness, optimism, calmness and wisdom* |
| **BROWN/BEIGE** | *Hesitation, uncertainty, neutrality, spiritual invisibility* |
| **PINK** | *Honor, true love, morality, innocence* |
| **BLACK** | *Mystery, self-discovery, change, beginnings and endings* |
| **PURPLE/VIOLET** | *Tension, ambition, business progress, power, concentration* |
| **SILVER/GREY** | *Cancellation, neutrality, stalemate* |
| **ORANGE** | *Encouragement, adaptability, stimulation, attraction, vitality, happiness, creativity* |
| **INDIGO** | *Insight, understanding, astral travel, inner and outer vision* |

*A*nother way to determine the proper color for you to focus on is by the zodiac. Each day of the week is governed by a particular zodiac sign; if you know that Thursday is governed by Jupiter, the planet of Sagittarius, the green of Jupiter or the red and gold of Sagittarius are good choices to wear on Thursday.

*H*ere are simple charts giving you colors for each day of the
week and each sign of the zodiac.

 Colors by Day

| Day | Planet | Color |
| --- | --- | --- |
| Sunday | Sun | Yellow or Gold |
| Monday | Moon | White or Silver |
| Tuesday | Mars | Red |
| Wednesday | Mercury | Purple |
| Thursday | Jupiter | Green |
| Friday | Venus | Blue |
| Saturday | Saturn | Black or Brown |

# Colors of the Zodiac

| Sign | Primary Color | Secondary Color |
| --- | --- | --- |
| Aquarius | Blue | Green |
| Pisces | White | Green |
| Aries | White | Pink |
| Taurus | Red | Yellow |
| Gemini | Red | Blue |
| Cancer | Green | Brown |
| Leo | Red | Green |
| Virgo | Gold | Black |
| Libra | Black | Blue |
| Scorpio | Brown | Black |
| Sagittarius | Gold | Red |
| Capricorn | Red | Brown |

# How to Calculate Your First Name Number

# Your First Name Number

*The symbolic significance*

*of your First Name Number*

*is very important. In fact, your first*

*name is what distinguishes you*

*from those who bear the same last*

*name as you. It represents your under-*

*lying, hidden nature. Most*

*important, it reveals what you must*

*bring out of the very depths of*

*your being to assert your personality*

*with total effectiveness. Your First*

*Name Number reveals your secret self*

*— the seed of your Success!*

As you've already seen, in numerology we only use the numbers from 1 to 9. Therefore, you must always reduce the totals you arrive at to a number between 1 and 9, inclusive. This is a hard-and-fast rule for all calculations.

*For example:*
*A total of 35 would be equivalent to*
*3 + 5 = 8.*

*Another example:*
*58 = 5 + 8 = 13.*
*And 13 = 1 + 3 = 4.*

To begin with, you must consult the following Astrological Love Number Table, which tells you which number represents each of the letters of the alphabet.

The Astrological Love Number Table is the basis for all the calculations you will be making for your First Name Number, so you will be referring to it each time you need to translate a letter to a number.

*Letters into Numbers*

| 1 | 2 | 3 | 4 | 5 | 6 | 7 | 8 | 9 |
|---|---|---|---|---|---|---|---|---|
| A | B | C | D | E | F | G | H | I |
| J | K | L | M | N | O | P | Q | R |
| S | T | U | V | W | X | Y | Z | |

*H*ere's how to find your First Name Number.

At this point, you may begin to work out your own First Name Number

in the work space provided or on your own paper.

*Example 1 ❖ John Smith*

| JOHN | Your Name |
|------|-----------|
| J = 1 | |
| O = 6 | |
| H = 8 | |
| N = 5 | |

*Step 2* ᨀ: Number each letter in the correct order, BUT STARTING FROM THE LAST. In other words, for the name "John," there are 4 letters. Instead of counting J = 1, O = 2, H = 3 and N = 4, count them backwards: J = 4, O = 3, H = 2 and N = 1. These numbers are called ORDER NUMBERS. Find the ORDER NUMBERS for your first name. Then multiply the ORDER NUMBER by the NUMBER from Table A for each of the letters. Then calculate the TOTAL of all the SUBTOTALS and reduce it to a single number.

$$J = 4 \times 1 = 4$$
$$O = 3 \times 6 = 18$$
$$H = 2 \times 8 = 16$$
$$N = 1 \times 5 = 5$$

*Total of Subtotals:*
$$4 + 18 + 16 + 5 = 43*$$
*Then:* $43 = 4 + 3 = 7$

## The FIRST NAME NUMBER
### is therefore 7

After you find your First Name Number, consult the following Interpretations to discover what your Number reveals about your secret self.

## 1.

As a Number 1, you are generally creative, an innovator and a pioneer. Inspired, determined, independent, you have a tendency to get satisfaction from the results obtained. Number 1, you are a born commander and organizer, but you often don't take circumstances into account. You won't put up with being distracted when your mind is set on something; your pride demands that you achieve your desired ends at any price. You are dominant, even to the point of egoism; nevertheless, you have a generous nature and can be very kind as long as you're getting your own way. A Number 1 is out of the ordinary, and you often rebel against work and family circles. Hardworking and energetic, you can become harsh and explosive. You have more admirers than friends and feel a strong "negative" rush toward anyone who is unjust or malicious towards you; you sometimes have difficulty forgiving and forgetting. In fact, you combine energy with great sensitivity, and you cultivate a harsh exterior to hide that sensitivity. Getting through that tough exterior is pretty difficult but can be easily done by those who show you that they care about you. Those people will uncover a warm friend in you. If they don't, you'll make them suffer, all the while suffering yourself because of your basic difficulty with communication.

## 2.

As a Number 2, you're a diplomat. You prefer success through hard work over risk or adventure. You are generally reserved, making decisions only after careful consideration. You need a harmonious atmosphere without any arguments or disagreement, so you sometimes have a tendency to bury your head in the sand to avoid coming to terms with life's difficulties. You dread any difficulty and in an unharmonious environment can become depressed. Your emotions dictate your actions more often than pure reason. While seemingly relaxed, you may often be quite tense, living in fear that everything around you will come apart. You can go from laughing to crying without apparent reason. You have many friends because you know how to listen, help, understand and comfort. You frequently embrace charitable or humanitarian causes. Number 2 is never vindictive and rarely gets angry. In a crisis, you're more likely to withdraw into yourself.

3. As a number 3, you are generally a good-humored and well-balanced person, but your anger can be surprising. You also are a good student. Enthusiastic, optimistic, and very energetic, you appreciate company and can be friendly and down to earth as well as profound. In general, people are happy being around you. Easily influenced by temporary conditions and (despite your ambitions) rarely dominating, you can seem immodest and self-centered when you can't suppress your enthusiasm. You appreciate money for the pleasures it can buy you more than to build up capital or invest it. You know how to take advantage of life's material pleasures. You are sociable and even popular, and you know how to give a party by creating a dynamic and fun-filled atmosphere. You have a lot of friends, but many of your friendships remain superficial. You are aware of the realities of life; still, your desire to be optimistic sometimes makes you bypass important moments because you are a bit afraid to show your deeper feelings.

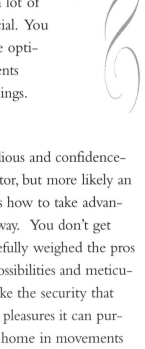

4. Number 4, you are a diligent, studious and confidence-inspiring worker. You are rarely an innovator, but more likely an adapter, an organizer, a builder who knows how to take advantage of the opportunities that come your way. You don't get involved with a project until you have carefully weighed the pros and cons, after having considered all the possibilities and meticulously mapped out a plan of action. You like the security that comes with having money rather than the pleasures it can purchase. You can't stand injustice and feel at home in movements that fight against any type of abuse. You appreciate peace, quiet

and discretion. You have few friends, but those few are loyal to you all their lives because you are a model of loyalty yourself. You won't put up with gossip and malicious rumors. You can sometimes demonstrate extreme tactfulness and diplomacy, but that is balanced by an extremely honest side that can be direct even to an extreme. This very rare and almost rude frankness only comes out when you've been pushed to your limits. You have an extraordinary capacity for stubbornness: you're capable of moving mountains to get what you want. You are addicted to work. You are also conservative for the most part and respectful of family traditions.

**5.** Number 5, you have a very quick temper which can affect the projects you undertake. You are enamored of freedom and often worry about losing yours. Sometimes you sacrifice a stable position you have attained only to throw yourself into some unknown adventure. You constantly question everything, and suffer greatly when you feel tied down by responsibility or circumstances not of your own choosing. You may then become nervous, irritable and sullen; however, you have staying power and can keep this sort of situation under control if you're on the watch for it. You act impulsively without making long-term plans, and like to take life as it comes, one day at a time. You can go suddenly from enthusiasm to despair, but these mood shifts are brief and you can get the upper hand on them. Money is mainly a means to pleasure for you. You're energetic, know how to make decisions and give as well as you get. Impulsive in both thought and deed, you're easily annoyed when anyone puts a spoke in your wheel. Despite everything, your natural charm attracts numerous friends, and makes you an excellent host at both social and professional gatherings and a powerful driving force within a small team or a larger group. You're creative and know how to make the best use of your skills. You have many acquaintances but few real friends due to your impetuous and impatient nature. To be your friend someone needs that very thing which you most often lack: patience.

6. Number 6, you are in general a faithful and trustworthy friend. You are noble and a lover of beauty in all things, and have a great sense of humanity, particularly when it comes to the family. Sometimes you tend to "go too far" and don't recognize limits of acceptability. You appear serene and charming and easily attract many friends. However, your unstable behavior may cause you to swing from the greatest gentleness to extreme anger, all because of your hypersensitivity. You love beautiful things, especially music. You really enjoy playing host to friends and organize social functions well in advance so they run smoothly and everyone has a genuinely good time. Generous and spontaneous, you may easily fall prey to unscrupulous people. Yours is a personality that goes its own sweet way without fuss, slowly but all the more surely for it. People are sometimes surprised at just how much you've achieved without them suspecting a thing.

7. Number 7, you are a thinker: analytical, independent and full of worries. Above all, you're very curious about all sorts of things. Self-sacrifice won't stop you from satisfying your curiosity — nor will the warnings of well-meaning friends who keep telling you what killed the cat. You find it hard to accept the opinions and judgment of others because

you want to see and understand for yourself. You like to travel, with discovery and knowledge as your main desires. Yet it's essential for you to make time to be alone. Generally introverted and studious, you appreciate the arts and all beauty in general. A perfectionist, you are rarely truly satisfied either by your own achievements or by what other people have to offer. You don't have a lot of friends, but to those you have and love, you are loyal, patient and generous. In any case, you prefer smaller groups rather than a "bunch of buddies." You may be interested by anything mysterious or occult, either because of curiosity or a thirst for spiritual fulfillment. Number 7, you are someone who wants to believe in something and who is forever searching for that something.

## 8.

Number 8, you possess huge powers of self-control and concentration. Like your will, your personality is distinct and very strong. You sometimes even prove fanatical in your commitments. You despise mediocrity and stinginess; that may put you on the road to glorious success but also may lead you into crushing defeat. You're hard on yourself and on others. You can be completely devoted to a cause or belief and can be surprised when other people don't feel the same. Often you appear cold and distant, while in truth you have trouble expressing your feelings, for under your firm mask you hide a warm personality. You really hope to gain the friendship of others but have trouble dropping your reserve. You're energetic and lively and always ready to participate in any research. Sometimes you exude a certain magnetism which attracts and fascinates others. Curiously, that doesn't stop you from feeling isolated because you're absorbed in your own projects and work. Also, you withdraw from people who don't interest you. On the other hand, you're ready to go out of your way for your real friends and for projects that really interest you. You're loyal but you never forget a betrayal and probably still harbor grudges from grade school. A stubborn fighter, you know how to combat your adversaries to the very end and to overcome any obstacles that life throws up along the way.

9. Number 9, you are always sensitive to the needs of others, especially those who suffer: victims, the oppressed, the ill or the underprivileged. Moreover, you are so impassioned by the fight against poverty that you may forget any problems in your own circle. On the other hand, rather than trying to solve important problems that bother you with intense action, you prefer a more philosophical approach or even the use of psychic or occult means. You seek power and money only to better help others. Vigorous, courageous and determined, in actuality, you only rarely use your talent. Your aim in life could be something akin to "Universal Love." You know how to incite the love of many with occasional lively and over-enthusiastic outbursts. You are sincerely excited by great debates. However, you can also be shy, distant and independent, you do little to facilitate communication with those around you. Also, you are prone to mood swings: one day very lively and enthusiastic, the next sad and gloomy. Despite this slightly complex personality, you never lose sight of your humanitarian aims.

# Your Self-Motivation Number

Another numerological formula that will enhance your success is the Self-Motivation Number, metaphysically called the "soul urge." This number describes how to achieve the kind of success you desire and ultimately want out of life.

# How to Calculate Your Self-Motivation Number

In the previous exercise, you derived your First Name Number from the number values of all the letters in your first name. However, calculating your Self-Motivation Number differs from calculating your First Name Number in two ways. Your Self-Motivation Number is concerned only with vowels, and takes into account the vowels of your entire birth name.

There is something magical about a name, and success can reveal itself to you if you agree to recognize the positive powers in a name. You add together the numerical equivalents for the vowels in your name and then reduce them to a single digit. So, use the entire name as it was first recorded on your birth certificate (however, do not include Junior, Senior, II, III, etc., or nicknames), and proceed in the following manner:

We are only concerned with the vowels in a name. A, e, i, o and u are vowels. Y becomes a vowel if a, e, i, o or u are not present in a syllable. The following numbers for the vowels in English are based on an ancient method of Numerology from Greece and Turkey. The other letters, the consonants, also have corresponding numbers, but they do not concern us here.

$$A = 1 \quad E = 5 \quad I = 9 \quad O = 6 \quad U = 3 \quad Y = 7$$

Write your name down on a piece of paper, clearly and with enough space to work. Remember to use the name on your birth certificate, not your nickname, and to drop any Jr., Sr., or other suffix. For an example, I am going to use the name of a former President of the United States, RONALD WILSON REAGAN.

*Step 1* ❧ *Find any vowels in your name and write the corresponding number beneath each vowel.*

RONALD WILSON REAGAN
*Step 1* ❧    **6      1      9      6      5      1      1**

*Step 2* ❧ *Next, total the numbers separately for the first, middle and last names. If any of those numbers add up to a two-digit number, add them together to reduce them to a single digit.*

RONALD WILSON REAGAN
*Step 1* ❧    **6      1      9      6      5      1      1**

*Step 2* ❧    **6 + 1 = 7      9 + 6 = 15      5 + 1 + 1 = 7      1 + 5 = 6**

*Step 3* ❧ *Then add the first, middle and last name numbers together to form a single number. Again, if necessary, reduce this number to a single digit. That digit is your Self-Motivation Number.*

RONALD WILSON REAGAN
*Step 3* ❧    **7 + 6 + 7 = 20      2 + 0 = 2**

Former President Reagan's Self-Motivation Number is 2. What is yours?

Now, read the meaning of your Self-Motivation Number in the following list and reflect on what you can learn from it to attain success in your chosen field.

# Self-Motivation Number Interpretations

**one**

Number 1: Strong-willed number 1's relish their freedom to control their own activities and rarely listen to the advice of others. Number 1's are comfortable in a leadership role, but prefer to leave the "nuts and bolts" details to a subordinate. They apply their formidable willpower, vigor, determination and perseverance to successfully get what they want. Once they have attained success, they will unfailingly try to improve on it.

**two**

Number 2: Sensitive number 2's are receptive to the feelings of others and generally shine in cooperative efforts. They are adaptable, supportive, easy-going, and diplomatic, and are more comfortable following than leading. They enjoy acquiring knowledge and information, and are good at absorbing a vast array of details.

**three**

Number 3: Creative, communicative Number 3's want to be popular and witty, and they thrive in social or professional situations where they can talk and interact with others. Often optimistic and slightly naive, they adore children and animals, and others are drawn to their cheerfulness and youthfulness. They may be quite impractical, but can use their extraordinary imaginative abilities to visualize their dreams.

**four**

Number 4: Reliable Number 4's are deliberate, industrious, and are especially good in positions dealing with structure, order and management. Dutiful and dependable, they enjoy traditional values, and exercise caution and prudence in their path to success. They are courteous, but may appear a bit rigid in their ideas.

**five**

Number 5: Entrepreneurial number 5's are curious, exciting, enthusiastic, and need to be constantly on the move. They enjoy being slightly unconventional and irresponsible. Spontaneous and energetic, they are often the catalysts for change in other people's lives. Number 5's find regimentation stifling and do best when given free rein.

Number 6: Well-intentioned number 6's like to be settled, judicious, and helpful. They have a tendency to be too tender-hearted and to want to fix everyone's problems. If left to their own devices, they will take on far too many projects. For this reason, they benefit from having their duties outlined for them. They enjoy beauty, comfort, and feeling needed.

*six*

Number 7: Visionary number 7's are perceptive, contemplative, mystical and erudite. Their ambitions usually reflect personal desires rather than commercial success. They are conscientious perfectionists and can easily become authorities on whatever subject catches their fancy. Highly impractical and other-worldly, they enjoy silence and do best when alone, lost in their own world. Number 7's are extremely uncomfortable in the noisy whirl of the modern business world.

*seven*

Number 8: Workaholic number 8's are serious about success. Their ambitions revolve around material wealth and possessions — they want to own and enjoy all that money can buy. Number 8's strive for influence, dignity and status. They have tremendous vitality, stamina and endurance, as they must to maintain their hectic schedules. They have minds like steel traps and are skillful manipulators and shrewd planners, so they do well in positions of leadership and problem-solving.

*eight*

Number 9: Noble number 9's appreciate wisdom and enjoy helping others and alleviating suffering. Thoughtful, empathetic and creative, they enjoy being involved in humanitarian or artistic projects of universal merit. Wealth and money hold no particular allure for number 9's; their rewards are more idealistic. They often become doctors, charity organizers, painters, writers and musicians. Above all, they want to live a worthwhile life.

*nine*

*Think of these self-motivation revelations as a springboard to higher success. You can use your new confidence and personal power to influence others, increase your leadership ability, and deal effectively with the power struggles that are inevitable in any quest for success.*

## ∴ Tarragon Success Sauce ∾

In French, tarragon means "little dragon." Perhaps the ancient powers of this mythical beast will help you attain personal power and success!

2 teaspoons finely chopped shallots
2 ounces fresh tarragon, chopped
1 ounce fresh chives, chopped
6 tablespoons vinegar

5 egg yolks
2 tablespoons water
3/4 pound sweet butter, melted
pinch salt & pepper

Combine the vinegar, shallots, chives, tarragon and salt in a small saucepan. Simmer until the liquid is reduced by half. Remove from heat; add 1 tablespoon cold water, egg yolks and pepper. Beat until thickened. Place over low heat. Mix in the butter a little at a time. Serve with chicken or fish.

*Magical Qualities* ∴ Power of myth and legend, invincibility, profound wisdom.

## ∴ Success Patties ∾

2 lbs. ground turkey
1/2 cup grated Parmesan cheese
1/2 cup grated romano cheese
1/2 cup minced fresh parsley
4 cloves garlic, minced
2 finely chopped bay leaves

1 tablespoon ground fennel
1/8 teaspoon red pepper
1 teaspoon pepper
1 teaspoon salt
4 tablespoons water

Combine all ingredients and form into patties. Place waxed paper between each patty and wrap well. Freeze. These patties are great to have on hand for unexpected visitors. Remove the number of patties you will need from the freezer and let thaw in the refrigerator. When they are thawed, pan-fry or grill them.

Success, achievement and mastery.

*Magical Qualities* ∴

# CHAPTER THREE

## Enchantments for Prosperity

*C*ontrary to what has been said
or written since the beginning of Time, Fortune is not blind.

❧

Fortune follows a very precise pattern and fills the pockets
of some people because they have an attitude towards life that is different from
that of the eternal loser. Indeed, they have faith and are bursting with positive
thoughts. Their subconscious is flooded with positive energy that brings them
abundance in whatever they ask for.

❧

If your attitude towards life is negative—if you constantly fear misfortune,
failure, and bad times—these things will surely descend upon you. This negative
attitude can be compared to the action of a lightning rod that attracts and catches
the lightning bolt. As long as you brandish this negative concept above your head,
you won't ever be a winner.

❧

You must emit positive thoughts of winning and wealth, without ever slowing
down or feeling doubt. Use these Enchantments for Prosperity and soon you will
plant positive thoughts in your subconscious that will germinate and grow into an
uninterrupted series of beneficial events that will transform your life with abun=
dance and wealth.

*Perhaps you are saying to yourself that you have many things to change in your financial outlook. It's often helpful to verbalize the most important ideas with short, precise sentences. So, the following Seven Prosperity Statements can help you enormously on your way towards abundance and wealth. These are affirmative visualizations that are going to program your consciousness with the specific goal of increasing your wealth.*

$ The following are seven statements to build prosperity. Repeat each statement ten times to yourself.

$ Make sure that you are really absorbing the statement and that it feels right to you. Take a deep breath, and let the statement nestle into your subconscious.

$ As you repeat these statements, notice how you breathe. With each inhalation, think, "My every breath draws money to me." With each exhalation, think, "My every breath repels negative thoughts from me."

$ Know in your heart that financial wealth stems from spiritual wealth. Your thoughts of abundance for yourself must be linked with thoughts of abundance for those around you.

$ Use the remarkable power of your imagination to envision yourself as happily wealthy. You may use any associations these statements suggest to you. Just enjoy yourself and, most of all, believe in yourself!

## Prosperity Statement Number 1:

*Money flows into my life like a stream into the ocean.*
*My spirit swims in a sea of Abundance.*

## Prosperity Statement Number 2:

*My mind is a never-ending fountain of valuable ideas.*
*I need only dip into it and drink deeply.*

## Prosperity Statement Number 3:

*I do only the work that I love and can do with joy. That love and joy*
*attracts all the money I need.*

## Prosperity Statement Number 4:

*I use my money generously for myself and those I love.*
*Every dollar I spend on others returns to me again and again, in love and joy.*

## Prosperity Statement Number 5:

*The money in my bank account grows and grows. It accumulates*
*for me to use at my pleasure.*

## Prosperity Statement Number 6:

*My worth increases every day. As my spirit grows,*
*so does my material and psychic value.*

## Prosperity Statement Number 7:

*All my experiences with money are positive and valuable.*
*There is no loss — there is only experience.*

The minerals with the most power over our lives are gold and silver. Even if we never see the real thing from day to day, most of us spend much of our existence thinking, worrying and planning about what gold and silver represent to us — *money*. Therefore, any money, even if it's made of paper or a plastic credit card, is governed by the power of gold and silver.

Over the centuries, money has, through the immense psychic power it exerts over our lives, attracted a category of magical lore unto itself. If you are wondering why you can never hold onto your money, why it is always "slipping through your fingers," perhaps you are not treating your money right. Here are some magical rules for the getting, holding, and spending of money.

* Always keep at least a few coins in your home when leaving for a journey or vacations. To do otherwise bodes ill.

* If you drop any money while at home, say, "Money on the floor, money at the door." Step on the money and pick it up; more will come to you.

* Finding money is quite fortunate, but to keep such money is thought to invite misfortune. Spend it as quickly as possible, and tell no one of its origin.

* Never leave the house without at least one coin in your pocket or handbag. The best charm of all is a bent coin or a coin pierced with a hole. Carrying one of these is both "lucky" and quite protective.

* If you must fold your bills, fold them towards you, for this indicates that money will come to you. Folding money away from you will result in its quick disappearance.

* Finding a coin minted in the year of your birth is an exceptionally fortunate blessing. This is one type of "found money" that should be retained. Safeguard it as a charm and never spend it.

* Before midnight on New Year's Eve, place a small amount of silver money somewhere outside. Retrieve it the next morning on New Year's day and your earnings during the next year will be greater than your bills.

* On New Year's Day, rub yourself with a silver coin for money all year.

* To ensure that you will always have money and friends, tie a string into a circle and keep it in your pocket, wallet or purse.

* If you are ever becalmed at sea, throw a coin into the water; the winds will immediately fill the sails.

* Hold a silver coin in your hand, look over your shoulder at the first star that appears at dusk, and make a wish.

* Turn over silver money on the night of the new Moon to secure prosperity.

* Dreaming of money for three nights in a row indicates that money will soon come to the dreamer.

* Counting your money too often means it will soon be gone.

* Rub a small green candle with powdered cloves. Place it and its holder on top of a new dollar bill. Three hours after sunset on a Thursday evening, light the candle and let it burn until it has gone out. The next day, bury the candle stub; rub the bill with powdered cloves and hide it in the house.

*F*or this spell, you need an agate with fossils
in it, which is the stone of increasing wealth (you can find one at
a new age store, a museum shop, or any store specializing in crystals),
and some seeds of the basil plant (basil is the plant of wealth).
When the Moon is new and the wind is blowing from the East,
go into your garden or prepare a pot for planting. Facing the East,
plant the basil seeds and bury the agate deep in the soil with the seeds.
Do not put the agate on top of the seeds or so close to them that they
will not grow. Remember to water, fertilize and care for your plants.
As your plants grow, so will your wealth.

One note: the basil is an annual plant, which means it will
die off after about a year. You may harvest your basil before it flowers,
use it in cooking (this will give your dishes an added magical zest!) and
perform the spell again, in the same pot with the same agate.
Don't wait until your first plant dies, or you may lose
hold of your new wealth.

# To Obtain Money

*You will need one white candle to represent yourself, one gold candle, one green candle and one red candle, and some incense.*

**Step 1** ⌁ Light altar candles and incense.

**Step 2** ⌁ Sit for a moment, meditate on your purpose and relax. Don't think about anything. Get clear in your mind just what you wish to accomplish.

**Step 3** ⌁ Light the white candle which represents you, thinking hard of yourself. Say: *"This candle represents me. As it burns, so burns my spirit."*

**Step 4** ⌁ Light the gold candle. Think hard of attraction, and say: *"This candle represents attraction. It works with and for me."*

**Step 5** ⌁ Light the green candle, thinking hard of money. As you light it, say: *"This candle represents the money I desire. It is as much as I need — no more, no less."*

**Step 6** ⌁ Light the red candle, thinking of the complete wish fulfilled. Say: *"This candle represents the Power and the Command to drive the money to me."*

**Step 7** ⌁ Pause a moment to reflect. Then say: *"As money is necessary to the fulfillment of our needs, so must we ever strive to obtain it. All should be earned or not received at all. My*

*need at present is intense. Draw, then, money to me. Let me find all that I shall need. Supply, now, to meet my urgent want. Let all work well for me. Let me have sufficiency. Let me no longer have want."*

**Step 8** ⌁ Think now of the wish fulfilled, and of now having the money. Think of it actually being in your possession. Say: *"This money now is mine. I hold it and have it, and now it fills my need. I have received it safely and am glad. Now all is well."*

**Step 9** ⌁ Sit quietly for five minutes and let the candles and incense burn.

**Step 10** ⌁ Say: *"As I have willed this, so may it be done."* At this point you may extinguish the flames in reverse order.

The ritual should be repeated the following day, moving the gold, green and red candles closer to the white one.

You will find that this ritual will bring you money when it is badly needed. It will not bring money just for the sake of having money.

# To Gain Prosperity

*In addition to incense, you need altar candles and a white candle to represent yourself, one candle each of gold, purple, green and orange.*

**Step 1** — Light altar candles and incense.

**Step 2** — Meditate on growing more and more prosperous through your own efforts.

**Step 3** — Light the white candle and, concentrating on yourself, say: *"This candle represents me, whose spirit and determination are as strong and true as this flame."*

**Step 4** — Light the gold candle, concentrating on attraction, confidence and gain, and say: *"Here is my confidence. It is such that it cannot but draw prosperity to me."*

**Step 5** — Light the purple candle, concentrating on progress and power, and say: *"This is the flame of power. It must be handled carefully. But if so handled it will reward its handler with wealth and prosperity beyond his dreams. It is progress."*

**Step 6** — Light first the green candle, concentrating on wealth and prosperity, then the orange candle, thinking hard of the attraction of this wealth to yourself, and say: *"Here are to be found the monies of the world.*

*Here is true prosperity: true wealth and good fortune."*

**Step 7** — Think now of your wish fulfilled. Imagine yourself living a life of wealth; imagine the generous and benificent acts you will be able to perform with your new wealth. Keep your mind away from selfish and greedy images; imagine comfort, even luxury for yourself, but not vindictiveness or spite towards anyone you are trying to "show up" — your motives must remain pure. Say: *"This prosperity now is mine. I hold it and have it, and now it fills my need. I have received it safely and am glad. Now all is well."*

**Step 8** — Sit quietly for five minutes and let the candles and incense burn.

**Step 9** — Say: *"As I have willed this, so may it be done."* At this point you may extinguish the flames in reverse order.

The ritual should be repeated the following day, moving the gold, purple and green candles closer to the white one.

*Attracting Prosperity with Moon Oil*

❧ You will want to make this oil on a Thursday when the Moon is waxing. Heat 2 oz. cooking oil until warm, but not boiling. Add 1 teaspoon each of cinnamon, ginger, vanilla (bean or extract only, not artificial flavoring) and orange peel. When the oil has been strongly scented, remove from heat and strain. If you want a stronger oil, add fresh ingredients to the scented oil and repeat steps. Store in airtight jar or bottle. You may also wish to add a drop of green olive oil for the base. It's best to think about how you'll use the oil before you tint it. You certainly don't want your boss to see a drop of green oil on your forehead when you ask him for a raise!

*Attracting Money*

❧ Choose a period when the Moon is waxing and when you have some quiet time to devote to this ritual. It is necessary that you establish a state of mental calmnesss and self-confidence in order for this ritual to be effective. You will need a little sesame oil and some incense. Before beginning, rub your palms with sesame oil, using your bare hands. As you rub your palms together, concentrate on how much you need and deserve money! With any excess oil, anoint your brow, your breast-bone and your navel.

❧ Now you are all ready to begin. Light the incense. Continue to concentrate on your goal and chant out loud over and over while you feel the intensity and power of your purpose grow:

> *In the name of the Moon,*
> *I am worthy of an increase.*

When you feel your powers have reached their peak, say out loud:

> *As I will this, so may it done!*

❧ Let the incense burn down to remind you of your actions and to waft the power of your ritual to the appropriate ears.

*You might also want to discover the benefits of the Magic Plants and Herbs for Prosperity. These herbs, flowers and plants have been used to attract money and happiness for centuries. Use these herbs in your favorite dishes, buy yourself a bouquet of red tulips if you feel your prosperity will-power flagging, or give a bouquet of Lilies-of-the-Valley to a friend who's temporarily in dire financial straits... and watch wealth and prosperity blossom before your very eyes!*

### ∿ MAGIC PLANTS AND HERBS FOR PROSPERITY ∿

| Plants & Flowers | Properties |
|---|---|
| **ASHTREE** | *Material riches* |
| **BERGAMOT** | *Attracts money* |
| **CAMELLIA** | *Riches, sumptuous gifts, joy* |
| **CLOVER (THREE-LEAF)** | *Luck in games of chance* |
| **DAISIES** | *Elevated feelings, inspiration* |
| **DANDELION** | *Attracts money and luck* |
| **FENNEL** | *Attracts money* |
| **LILY OF THE VALLEY** | *Stimulates intellect and attracts money* |
| **MAPLE** | *Sociability, riches, work* |
| **OAK** | *Protection, vitality, health, riches* |
| **OATS** | *Energy, vitality, material prosperity* |
| **SARSAPARILLA** | *Social elevation, work, riches* |
| **TULIPS (RED)** | *Will-power* |

| Herbs | Properties |
|---|---|
| **BASIL** | *Protection, mental clarity, higher spiritual faculties* |
| **GINSENG** | *Riches, prosperity, vitality, sexual force* |
| **ROSEMARY** | *Happiness* |
| **SAGE** | *Protection, healing, luck and prosperity* |
| **THYME** | *Riches, health* |

# ❦ Green Abundance ❧

1 lb. lean pork, cooked and cubed
3 cups shredded green cabbage
4 potatoes, chopped
1 green pepper, chopped
2 cups chopped broccoli
12 whole Brussels sprouts
3 green onions with tops, diced

4 leeks, chopped
3 cloves garlic, minced
1/2 teaspoon dried thyme
1 teaspoon dried basil
1/2 teaspoon dried oregano
1/2 cup red wine
2 quarts water

Place all ingredients in a large pot. Simmer at least 2 hours.

*Magical Qualities* ❦ Financial growth, prosperity.

# ❦ Popovers of Prosperity ❧

*Basic Popover:*
2 eggs
1 cup flour
1 cup milk
1/2 teaspoon salt

*Filling:*
2 cups frozen chopped spinach, thawed
1 cup finely diced broccoli
1 teaspoon minced fresh parsley
1 tablespoon butter
1/2 teaspoon salt

Preheat oven to 450°F. Generously grease 6 custard dishes or muffin tins. Beat the eggs, flour, milk and salt until smooth, but do not overbeat. Fill the dishes or tins half full and bake for 20 minutes. Decrease temperature to 350°F and bake for 20 minutes more. Then remove popovers from dishes or tins immediately.

While the popovers are baking, prepare the filling. Place the spinach, broccoli, and parsley in a small saucepan with 1 inch of water. Cover and simmer for 3 minutes. Drain thoroughly. Add the butter and salt. Gently open or split the popovers and spoon filling into them. As you're filling the popovers, visualize your own pockets or bank account filling up with "green," too!

*Magical Qualities* ❦ Abundance, Prosperity and Success.

# CHAPTER

## FOUR

# Enchantments for Health

*The world shines with beauty
when you are glowing with good health.
Many people think of "health" as purely a physical question,
but being in good health means more than just being free of aches
and pains.  It also means feeling happy emotionally
and joyful spiritually.*

❧

*In this sense, your efforts to attain Love,
Success and Abundance in the previous chapters of this book
have been laying the groundwork for a solid sense of health
and well=being.  There's no better tonic to heal the body
and uplift the spirit than attaining
your deepest desires!*

❧

*For physical complaints, however,
the healing powers of herbs and home remedies
have been acclaimed for thousands of years.  Cultures all over
the world confirm that Mother Nature is really the best doctor of all!
In this section, you'll discover valuable secrets of Nature's "pharmacy,"
as well as how to use the Moon's magic to enjoy vibrant health
and radiant well=being every day.*

*Everywhere in the past, home remedies were used to treat a variety of illnesses and conditions.*

*Though each family knew some cures or treatments, many villages had at least one wise woman who charmed burns, dispensed medicinal potions and offered a shoulder on which to cry.*

*These wise women where anything but amateurs and in fact were often more skilled than the "doctors" who intermittently roamed the countryside. They knew the fundamentals of diagnosis and treatment, psychology, midwifery and a host of related disciplines. Many of the cures that they discovered were later accepted and used by established medical practitioners.*

*Not bound by religious conventions, these wise women freely mixed magic with medicine so as to strengthen the cure. Herbal medicines were compounded and applied with care and with an awareness of power. Used together, they often effected a cure, or at least relief.*

*Please take note that these remedies are not "one-dose cures" as you are used to having in regular medicine. When you use herbal teas, you must drink at least three cups a day for several days for the medicine to have any effect.*

 ## Colds:

Ginger is a wonderful plant for fighting the common cold, both as a prevention and as a cure. Ginger stimulates oxygenation of the blood and acts as a decongestant and disinfectant.

*Recipe:* Boil some water containing crushed ginger. Add honey and lemon to taste (you can also use ginger powder.)

Rose hips are an important natural source of Vitamin C. Yarrow is a strong fever reducer and detoxifies the system. Peppermint can be used with any herb combination to improve flavor, but it also has some curative value of its own.

*Recipe:* A tea made from yarrow blossoms steeped with peppermint, rose petals and rose hips will keep a cold from coming on. Drink as many cups a day as possible, but use the same yarrow blossoms several times over. Too much yarrow can make you dizzy.

Garlic is also a classic remedy for the common cold.

*Recipe:* Cut a few cloves into slices and place them on a piece of buttered bread or toast. If you don't like eating large amounts of garlic, take garlic capsules (they have no odor).

*Recipe:* A tea made from licorice root, blue vervain and echinacea root will ease a bad cough. Boil the licorice and echinacea together for several minutes, then turn off the heat and add the blue vervain leaves and some peppermint for flavor. Let the tea steep for five minutes, covered, then strain. Add lemon and honey to taste.

Coltsfoot and wild cherry bark is a good combination to ease bronchitis and congestion.

# ❧ Minor Burns:

Prepare a compress using one of the following substances:

*Recipe:* This plant, which you can easily grow in your house or apartment, is fittingly called the "burn plant." Aloe Vera creams are very effective, but using jelly from the fresh plant itself is even better. So the ideal thing is to keep a living plant in your house all the time.

*Recipe:* Place a piece of gauze over the wound, apply a half-inch clay compress and leave for one hour. Change the compress every 2 hours, even during the night.

*Recipe:* Steep the blossoms of calendula (pot marigold) in a cloth, then apply the cloth to the burn. Calendula is also good for wounds.

# ❧ Headaches:

*Compress:* Puree 2 onions and mix them with olive oil and salt. Prepare a compress and apply to the painful area.

*Essential oil:* Massage your temples with a couple of drops of essential oil of lavender and rosemary.

*Plants:* Eat raw or cooked fennel. Fennel is reputed to cure headaches caused by bad digestion.

*Teas:* A tea of peppermint and chamomile is a wonderful and tasty headache relief. White willow bark and valerian root is a stronger combination, good for migraines, but should not be used by those sensitive to aspirin.

## Insect Bites, Poison Ivy & Other "Itches":

Grind up the leaf of the common plantain until it becomes a paste and apply directly to the affected area.

## Stomach Aches:

*Essential oil:* Take with honey a number of times a day: Lemon, 5 to 10 drops; peppermint, 2 to 5 drops.

*Vegetable juice:* Drink a tablespoon of cabbage juice before meals and a tablespoon of raw potato juice after meals.

*Teas:* The all-purpose peppermint-chamomile tea is a fine way to ease an upset stomach. For upset stomach with gas, use a combination of anise seed, cayenne, dill seed, fennel seed and ginger root. Take it with meals.

*Other Remedies:* Chew a few almonds before eating and eat raw or cooked cabbage every day.

## Teeth:

*Mouth Care:* Certain preventive measures can help maintain healthy teeth. Eat myrtle, wild berries and oranges when in season. Wash your mouth frequently with a decoction of figs: 2 ounces of figs to 4 ounces of water.

*Toothaches:* Place a clove or a drop of essential oil of cloves on the aching tooth. Massage your cheek with a drop of rosemary or lavender essential oil.

Here is a chart of selected common herbs used for healing and magic. You can try to concoct your own recipes to suit your personal needs. Remember to be cautious about dosages, and never to ingest a plant whose properties you don't know. If you want more information about healing or magical herbs, there are many books on the subject that go into more detail.

## Herbs for health

| Herb | Parts to Use | Medicinal Properties | Magical Properties |
|------|-------------|---------------------|-------------------|
| *Anise* | Fruits (called seeds) | Good for digestion and in case of insomnia or nervousness | Awakens subtle energies needed for magic |
| *Balm* | Flowery tops and leaves | Digestive, sedative, good for "female complaints" and the complexion | Soothes away hurts and fears related to love |
| *Basil* | Flowery tops and leaves | Anti-inflammatory, appetizer, antiseptic, anti-spasmodic | Brings wealth |
| *Burdock* | Roots and leaves | Diuretic, purgative, antiseptic | Used for cleansing away low self-esteem |

| Herb | Parts to Use | Medicinal Properties | Magical Properties |
|------|--------------|---------------------|--------------------|
| Chamomile | Flowers | Digestive, sedative, a wash for sores, wounds and eyes | Prepares the mind for magic |
| Hawthorn | Flowers and fruits | Normalizes blood pressure, regulates the skin | Brings peace. Brings happiness and success at work |
| Mallow | Flowers and leaves | Treats inflammations and irritations of respiratory passages and eyes | Softens harsh characters and brings appreciation of natural beauty |
| Marjoram | Flowery tops | Aromatic, digestive, sedative for headaches and cramps | Traditionally accompanies the dead. Helps you accept loss and change |
| Mint | Flowery tops and leaves | Tonic for nervousness, tension headaches, stomachaches and cramps | Takes heat off excessive emotions and situations |
| Mugwort | Rootstock and leaves | Appetizer, digestive, sedative | Protects while traveling |
| Nettle | Top of plant | Diuretic, purifier, eases inflammation of the digestive tract | Resolves uncomfortable, "prickly" situations: jealousy, gossip, etc. |
| Rosemary | Leaves | Antiseptic, antispasmodic, stimulant, good for hair | Brings contentment and love |
| Skullcap | Whole plant | Eases spasms, convulsions, restlessness, brings on menstruation | Helps relax |
| Thyme | Leaves | Expectorant, antiseptic, stimulates appetite, eases gastritis, makes a good mouthwash | Inspires courage and strength |
| Valerian | Rootstock | Hypnotic, sedative, anti-neuralgic | Promotes dreams and reconciliation |
| Vervain | Whole plant | Astringent, diuretic, digestive, purifier | Leads to a new love |
| Witch hazel (DO NOT INGEST!) | Leaves | Astringent, decongestant, good for skin | Brings charm. Makes user irresistible |

# To Retain or Regain Health

In addition to altar candles, a white candle to represent yourself,
and incense, you will need one orange candle and three red candles. Arrange the
candles with the white in the center, the orange to the left and the three
reds in a vertical line to the right.

It is best to do this ritual on a Friday.

**Step 1** ⌁ Light altar candles and incense.

**Step 2** ⌁ Sit for a few moments, imagining yourself bursting with health. If you are ill, imagine new good health flowing into you like a river of light.

**Step 3** ⌁ Light the white candle and say: *"This candle is my spirit, in excellent health. May I be blessed that I may prosper."*

**Step 4** ⌁ Light the orange candle and say: *"This flame draws all that is good to me. Health and strength and all I desire."*

**Step 5** ⌁ Light the red candles. Say: *"Here is health and strength, three times over. May this be taken into my body, to help and serve me as I wish."*

**Step 6** ⌁ Imagine yourself healthy and strong. See the good life you will enjoy. Say:

*"As it is was ever thus. To live, one must have strength. One must have health. Strength to the weak, health to the weak. My own spirit will heal me. So may it be."*

**Step 7** ⌁ Think now of your wish fullfilled. Say: *"This new Health now is mine. I hold it and have it, and now it fills my need. I have received it safely and am glad. Now all is well."*

**Step 8** ⌁ Sit quietly for five minutes and let the candles and incense burn.

**Step 9** ⌁ Say: *"As I have willed this, so may it be done."*

Repeat this ritual every Friday for as long as necessary, moving the red and orange candles closer to the white each time, until they almost touch.

**Purifying Your Body With the Moon**

This method is good for cleansing your body. If you are someone who has problems with your blood sugar, then you will want to consult with your doctor before trying this method. Before beginning this exercise you will need to know the times of the New Moon and Full Moon. You can usually find this information in the Weather section of your newspaper.

As you will begin with the New Moon, verify the time period when it begins. For the 12 hours before and for the 12 hours after the time of the New Moon, don't eat anything, and only put liquids in your body. Don't worry if the New Moon starts at a strange hour and causes you to interrupt your normal schedule. For a change, disrupt your habits — it will keep you from becoming a fuddy-duddy who is so set in his ways. Of course, when I tell you to drink only liquids, don't think that milkshakes and alcohol are acceptable! The best liquids for you to drink are the following: 1½ liters of water (mineral water if you prefer) and herbal tea. Repeat this process 15 days later, on the Full Moon.

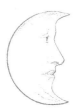

You will be shocked at how good you feel from this cleansing! If you don't believe me and find this method a little simplistic, just try it! You certainly don't have anything to lose, except feeling good about your body and those newly shed pounds. Try it for a few months and you will immediately see the difference. What is good about this method is that you practice it only 2 days a month. Of course, the rest of the time you need to eat moderate, balanced meals.

## Sleeping Well With the Moon

Perform this ritual every Full Moon. Scrape off the rind from a ripe lemon. Put your scrapings aside on a ceramic plate and let them dry for seven nights. Go outside and take the plate, a piece of white cloth cut into a small square, and a threaded needle. With just the light of the Moon, transfer the dried lemon peel to the center of the cloth. Fold the cloth in half, in the shape of a triangle. Stitch the two open sides together with your threaded needle. When finished, hold your little sachet up to the Moon and say the following words: *The charm is made.*

Put you creation under your pillow for a peaceful night's sleep. Keep this sachet under your pillow and see how your sleep patterns evolve. If necessary, repeat at the next Full Moon.

On a night of a Full Moon, gather the following ingredients: 1 cinnamon stick, a pinch of saffron, a handful of fresh rose petals, a piece of red sandalwood and 2 Tbsp. of aloe, 2 cups olive oil, 8-inch white candle. Only use real, fresh ingredients, never synthetics or substitutes. Add these ingredients to the warmed olive oil. Warm mixture until rose petals are translucent, then strain and add candle. When candle is melted, remove wick. Beat mixture until it attains a creamy mixture.

Store in airtight container. Anoint your forehead, breastbone and navel or pulse points (the neck or wrists) before going to bed on any of the following nights: Tuesday (the day of Mars), Thursday (the day of Jupiter) and Saturday (the day of Saturn). Perform this ritual once a year.

## Long Life Moon Elixer

# Secret 1 ∴ Overcome Anxiety

There is nothing wrong with worrying. It is a natural phenomenon that keeps us prepared for unexpected crises. This mental process comes from the time that humanity had just come down from the trees. It was necessary to keep a constant eye out for predators and natural disasters, so mankind developed the unique ability to ask ourselves, "What shall I do if the worst occurs?" It is this ability that has let our species survive for so long.

However, sometimes modern people worry too much. That is when, learned doctors say, you must learn that it is all right to worry, but only at the right time. Some people who suffer from anxiety find that doing a daily 20-minute "worry session" helps them keep their anxiety from running their lives.

If you find yourself worrying too much, make a mental list of all your worries every day. Then, at the same time and place each day, do nothing but worry. Yes! For 20 minutes every day, you may not think of anything but your worries. Pour them out. Exaggerate them to the point of absurdity. Think of the absolute worst thing that can happen to you, and then expand on it. Don't just imagine that you'll lose your job over an argument with your boss; imagine that after you lose your job, you get thrown out of your apartment because you can't pay your rent, and your wife leaves you because you can't support her, and you end up alone and unloved, sleeping on the curb... and then a car full of laughing teenagers comes along and splashes mud all over your only coat.

Silly, isn't it? In other words, make a caricature of the part of yourself that is always worried and exorcise it. Eliminating anxiety from your life will help prevent numerous psychosomatic illnesses such as ulcers and colitis.

# Secret 2 — Walk Away from Aging

Did you know that just walking for 30 minutes, 3 or 4 times
a week, is enough to combat aging?

It's said that one of the principal causes of the body's deterioration
as it ages is its diminished ability to break down and get efficient use of the food we eat.
However, this process, known as "glucose metabolization," can be kept functioning
smoothly by even leisurely exercise, like taking a walk.

Do you spend your whole day sitting at a desk
or in front of a computer screen? Why not get up occasionally and do a few minutes of
physical exercise? Don't worry about what other people think — chances are they wish
they had the guts to follow your lead. In fact, it's possible you could get a bunch of your
co-workers together for some group exercise.

That's exactly what they do in Japan, by the way.
In one Tokyo office, for example, every 40 minutes a bell sounds and everybody
gets up to do some quick stretching exercises together. Then they sit down again as
if nothing had happened. It relaxes the workers, gives everyone a break, and Japanese
managers say they're convinced it makes the workers more productive
and less likely to be absent due to illness.

# Secret 3 — Stimulate Your Immune System

Japanese seaweed possesses remarkable immunizing properties,
especially in fighting cancer. There are six types of seaweed that inhibit the growth
of colon cancer cells in rats, especially two types of the species Laminaria. Laminaria
extract has been proven by Japanese researchers to be up to 80% effective in

suppressing intestinal tumors. Wakame, another effective Japanese seaweed, is more commonly available in the West due to its importance in macrobiotic cuisine.

By the way, another reputed benefit of eating seaweed is the inhibition of male pattern baldness. That's right — Japanese folk doctors swear that eating seaweed can prevent hair loss in men. So the next time someone offers you sushi or miso soup, think twice before refusing. You may be denying yourself a health benefit.

## Secret 4 ∴ Prevent Motion Sickness

Fishing peoples have used these techniques to defeat seasickness, but you can use them for any incident of queasiness or upset stomach.

Did you know that half a teaspoon of common ground ginger is more effective than any chemical in preventing nausea? If taken for motion sickness, ingest the ginger 20 minutes before you travel. Avoid caffeine, alcohol, spicy food and other stimulants, and you should be fine.

Another method that is quickly gaining acceptance in the West is to place some form of pressure on the inside of your wrist. This is the location of a traditional acupressure point that inhibits the vomiting reflex. It is located a distance of two finger widths from the place where the hand and wrist meet. Many boating or outdoor stores sell premade "seasickness straps" that locate the pressure point for you.

## Secret 5 ∴ Painless Weight Loss

Acupressure is a fascinating subject! In fact, there is an acupressure weight-loss technique that only requires wearing a string around your right forearm.

According to folk doctors, a gentle but constant pressure
on the nerves of the forearm stimulates certain glands, particularly those such as
the thyroid and superadrenals that are involved in metabolism control.

Try an experiment for yourself. Find two ordinary rubber bands
and place them around your forearm, one–third of the way up from your wrist to
your elbow. The rubber bands should exert noticeable pressure without cutting off
blood circulation, and should not slip or slide when you move your arm.
It is not a tourniquet!

For best results, wear the bands constantly, even when you sleep.
It is also recommended not to wear any other jewelry on your right arm.

# Secret 6 ∿: Miracle Cure #1?

Not all health secrets come from the far corners of the globe.
The major proponents of what may well prove to be the world's miracle cure-all
come from California, USA. This common substance can prevent asthma, allergies,
common colds and flus, reduce cholesterol and menstrual cramps, increase the
absorption of iron and thereby increase your energy level... and some people say
it can even prevent cancer.

What is it? It's Vitamin C, commonly found in citrus fruits,
tomatoes, potatoes, green leafy vegetables, green peppers, strawberries, melon, and
other familiar foods.

Everyone knows that it's best to take large doses of Vitamin C in the winter to
help prevent colds and flus. Studies have also shown that taking at least 1 gram (1000
milligrams) of the vitamin every day can reduce the frequency of asthma attacks. Allergy
sufferers should start with a dose of 3 grams at the onset of an attack and take another 1
or 2 grams every 3 hours until the symptoms disappear.

If you are combatting the effects of cholesterol, start with 2 grams a day,
in concert with brewer's yeast and lecithin. Vitamin E will also help in this regard.

A dose of 2 grams of Vitamin C, along with 50 milligrams of Vitamin B-6 and a combination of 1 gram of calcium and 500 milligrams of magnesium (always take these two together) will decrease the intensity of menstrual pain. As long as you are taking this for menstrual pain, you might also want to take an iron supplement. Loss of hemoglobin during menstruation is a common cause of fatigue among women, and the Vitamin C doubles the amount of iron your body absorbs, so you may as well take advantage of it.

The medical mainstream still hasn't accepted the power of Vitamin C to fight cancer, but two-time Nobel Prizewinner Linus Pauling is convinced that large doses of this vitamin (5 grams or more daily) prevents tumor growth and bolsters the body's immune system.

If you smoke tobacco, spend a lot of time in traffic or take oral contraceptives, it is a good idea to increase your intake of Vitamin C. Inhaling carbon monoxide and increasing the estrogen in your body are two things that cause Vitamin C deficiency.

But taking the large doses of the vitamin recommended here does have side effects. You may want to watch out for nausea and diarrhea. Be sure to drink lots of water during the day to keep your system flushed, and drink no caffeine or alcohol. Cups of chamomile tea will also reduce these symptoms.

# Secret 7 ∿ Miracle Cure #2?

If someone offered you a miracle remedy that prevents cardiac disease, certain types of cancer, diabetes, obesity, tooth decay and varicose veins, would you buy it? Certainly you would.

There is such a product, and it's not a recent discovery. You won't find it in a pharmacy but in a grocery store. It's fiber.

Studies have shown that subjects with a low-fiber diet are 3 times more susceptible to life-threatening disease — no matter the cause — than those whose diet contains a lot of fiber.

Again, the medical mainstream is reluctant to admit that such a simple cure can prevent all the diseases I've mentioned, but there is conclusive proof that societies with a low-fiber diet, such as the United States, have a higher incidence of such serious medical problems.

For example, the diet of Eastern European countries is rich in whole grains, cabbage, potatoes, beans and lentils, and we would do well to follow their example. The simple, common "peasant" dish of rice and beans is prepared in numerous ways in many different countries; it is inexpensive and nutritious, offering a great amount of fiber and protein for very little money.

No one is saying you must limit your diet, though. A diet containing 37 grams of fiber a day (the equivalent of one cup of bran, one apple, one potato and half a cup of cooked spinach) can be obtained in many different ways while effectively protecting you against many illnesses common to modern western society.

Low–fiber foods include processed white bread, beef, pork, chicken, milk, butter, cheese, sugar, processed meats, desserts, fish, seafood and noodles. It is not necessary to avoid these foods entirely; some of them offer proteins that are essential for other body processes. Just don't form your diet entirely from these items.

Good sources of fiber include fruits, especially apples and prunes; vegetables, including potatoes with the peel on, artichokes, cabbage and peas; whole grains, such as barley, whole wheat (because of the bran it contains, which is why you should eat whole wheat bread), oats, corn, bulgar wheat, brown rice; nuts such as peanuts, walnuts and almonds; dried fruits like raisins, prunes, figs and dates; and legumes, including soy, beans, lentils and chick peas. Keep a selection of fiber-rich foods at hand and enjoy the variety.

# Secret 8 ⌁ Love to Live

Did you know that sexual activity can keep you looking good as you age? Studies conducted in Sweden have shown that elderly people who have sexual partners have much more vitality and a better memory than those who do not.

So don't let your golden years deprive you of the pleasures of sex! Just forget about the obsession of having to "perform." The final result is less important than the stimulation itself.

# ◦: *Chrysanthemum Chicken* :◦

In China, the chrysanthemum flower is the symbol of long life, invigoration and health.

4 white chrysanthemum blossoms,
   chopped
1 onion, chopped
1/4 cup butter
3 cups croutons
1 cup cooked long–grain rice

1 cup cooked spinach, chopped
1/2 cup finely chopped cabbage
2 tablespoons soy sauce
1/2 teaspoon 5-spice powder (available
in Asian groceries)
1 (3-lb) roasting chicken

Preheat the oven to 350°F. Sauté the chrysanthemums and onions in the butter until the onions are tender. Combine the croutons, rice, spinach, cabbage, five-spice powder and soy sauce. Mix in the sauteed items. If the stuffing is dry, add a little water. Stuff the chicken. Make a slit at the top of the bird and place a dollop of butter inside. Place the chicken in a roasting pan; add 1/4 inch water. Roast for 2 hours, basting frequently.

*Magical Qualities* ◦: Vitality, health, well-being.

# ◦: *Ginger Vinaigrette* :◦

1/2 cup olive oil
1/2 teaspoon ground ginger
1 tablespoon wine vinegar

Salt
Pepper

Warm the oil and ginger in a small saucepan over low heat. Stir in the vinegar, salt and pepper. Chill. This vinaigrette is delicious over cucumber slices, but try it also over other raw vegetable salads.

*Magical Qualities* ◦: Health and purification.

*I* hope you've enjoyed discovering the
Secrets of the Enchanted Unknown. Once you've glimpsed
the many magical powers of the natural world,
you will never look at life the
same way again!

❧

My fondest wish is that these secrets
will help make your dreams come true — that you will find
or deepen your true love, that you will enjoy the success
and prosperity you deserve, and that you will always feel
full of joy and vigor.

❧

You see, when you open your eyes and your spirit
to the magic around you, the world truly is an
enchanting place!

# NOTES

# NOTES

NOTES

# NOTES